Zumikon Residence

THE MONACELLI PRESS

Zumikon Residence

Gwathmey Siegel

Introduction by Charles Gwathmey

Architect	Gwathmey Siegel & Associates Architects
	Bruce Donnally (associate in charge)
	Nancy Clayton (project architect)
	Tom Lewis, Sylvia Becker, Carole Iselin (project team)
Associate Architect	Pfister + Scheiss Architekten
	Tom Pfister, Rita Scheiss (principals)
	Daniela Staub (project architect)
	Heinz Aebi (construction manager)

First published in the United States of America in 1996 by
The Monacelli Press, Inc.,
10 East 92nd Street, New York, New York 10128.

Library of Congress Cataloging-in-Publication Data
Zumikon Residence : Gwathmey Siegel / introduction by Charles Gwathmey.
p. cm. — (One house)
ISBN 1-885254-28-8 (pbk.)
1. Zumikon Residence (Zumikon, Switzerland). 2. Architecture, Postmodern—Switzerland—Zumikon.
3. Gwathmey Siegel & Associates Architects. 4. Bechtler, Thomas—Homes and haunts—Switzerland—Zumikon.
5. Zumikon (Switzerland)—Buildings, structures, etc. I. Gwathmey, Charles, 1938– .
II. Gwathmey Siegel & Associates Architects. III. Series.
NA7393.Z82Z86 1996
728'.372'0949457—dc20   96-5620

Printed and bound in Italy

Designed and composed by *Group* **C** Inc New Haven/Boston
Edited by Brad Collins

Zumikon Contents

Introduction
Charles Gwathmey

In the spring of 1990, Thomas Bechtler, a Swiss businessman and art collector, called me out of the blue, introduced himself and said he was coming to the United States. He wanted to build a house in Zumikon, a small village fifteen minutes from central Zurich, and was considering three architects—Gwathmey Siegel, Richard Meier and Tadao Ando—all modernists.

We met in New York and spent almost two hours talking. A vital part of our conversation was an objective and frank discussion of the similarities and differences he and I perceived in the work of the three architects. He was knowledgeable and committed to the idea of the modern movement as an essential component of the history of art and architecture. We shared an empathy and an immediate rapport that was irrefutable. Toward the end of our conversation I suggested we visit the Guggenheim Museum, which was under construction. He found it intriguing, and as we said our goodbyes, I had a positive sense about our meeting.

Two days later, he called and said he'd reached a decision: he asked if I would come to Zurich to meet his wife, Cristina, and their children, visit the site and discuss the project in more detail.

On my initial trip, Thomas and Cristina made it clear that they did not want a "house"; they wanted a work of architecture that would accommodate their family and their art. There was no hesitation, no insecurity or compromise. A reductive essentialism was a mutual mandate. The dialogue was uplifting and endured throughout the process. There was a climate of mutually collaborative discovery that was open and unencumbered by insecure habitual notions of "house." They were the ideal client/patron.

The evening before I returned to New York on that first trip, Thomas and Cristina hosted a dinner to introduce me to their friends and to announce their plans to build a new house. The camaraderie was infectious and Thomas's toast to the future, his unhesitating trust and his affection were genuine and moving. I was grateful and slightly unnerved, feeling a positive pressure and expectation that were uniquely motivating. I was determined to fulfill our shared aspirations to build a house of consequence, not a Swiss house or an American house, but an enduring work of architecture.

Bruce Donnally, our associate in charge of the project, and I returned to Zurich six weeks later with a wood mass/site model and plans that consolidated the parti. When we reviewed the scheme with the Bechtlers, their reception was so positive that I suggested we immediately present it to the town zoning director and building inspector.

The scheme incorporated the Bechtler's programmatic requirements and aspirations. It also addressed the constraints posed by the local planning and zoning regulations:

> The first constraint, one we had never encountered with any house we had designed before, was the necessity of maintaining the existing site topography. This automatically mandated that the scheme be integrated into the sloping hillside, obviously affecting the section and, when the program was overlaid, the vertical organization of the building.

> The second constraint was that the roof eave line could not measure more than 4.5 meters above the corresponding point in the land. This reinforced the relationship between the section and the topography and had a huge impact on the overall disposition of the building.

> The third constraint was that the square footage of the house was determined by a proportional relationship to the area of the site. Underground space, however, was not considered part of the livable or measured space of the building.

We knew that our house was unique in its organization, its code interpretation and aesthetic. The predominant architecture of Zumikon is half-timber stucco buildings—not old but definitely referential—with wood-frame farm buildings on the perimeter.

We presented the model and plans, describing the house as a reinterpretation of a village. The zoning director and building inspector were intrigued and appreciated being included at this early stage. They approved our initiating the formal town approval process. The following text and model photographs were submitted for the vote:

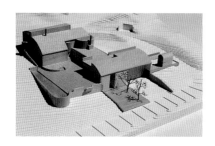

During the design of the Zumikon Residence two goals were in the foreground: first to create a relationship to the site that respects the historic significance of Zumikon, and second, to integrate the architecture into a terrain in such a way that both create a harmonious entity.

Inspired by roof silhouettes, village squares and gardens, the house is divided into four related building elements. Each of these elements is self-sufficient, supporting the idea that the composition as a whole is a microcosm of a village.

The first of the four elements is located near the street and consists of the entry, garage, kitchen/breakfast room and guest room. Its upper floor connects the service entry area and the second building element, the large terrace. This exterior space has two levels and integrates the swimming pool. The terrace is the heart of the house and can be conceptually compared to a "piazza" or "village square."

The third element of the house consists of a gallery and dining room above which is a roof garden with a sculpture terrace. This roof terrace is the most important connection between the front and back parts of the building.

The fourth element, located at the rear on the sloping side of the site, encompasses the living room, library, master bedroom, studio and "children's house," the forms and roofs of which are articulated in such a way that the parti of the village is reiterated formally.

The arrangement of the elements and their composition is directly related to the natural topography of the site. The grouping of interconnected building elements and exterior spaces integrates completely into the existing context and consequently enters into a sympathetic dialogue with the natural environment and the village.

As a result of the restrictive zoning ordinance for sloping sites, the house was designed as a series of stepping, interconnected, small scale articulated building elements. Together, those represent a "village-on-a-slope" whose origins can be traced to the context of Zumikon and to the rich architectural heritage of Switzerland.

We are convinced that this house is a serious and important architectural project which, commissioned by a patron of the arts, is dedicated to the excellence and future of your community. We hope that our proposal will satisfy you and that you will give it your support.

It is interesting that the final building varied so slightly, formally, from the original site model. I knew when we arrived at this scheme that we had not only satisfied all the zoning constraints; but that the parti was resolved.

This was the first house we had designed with an art collection as an integral part of the program. The Bechtler family has a tradition of art collection and patronage. Thomas and Cristina collect modern sculpture, particularly the work of Richard Long. As part of their initial requirements they wanted not only to display Long's ground work circular forms in a dedicated gallery space, but to integrate a fresco hand-painting into a major wall of the house as well.

Though this latter condition did not drive the section of the living space, the idea of "wall" did become a conscious and integrated part of the design. The solid-void articulation concentrated on accommodating the art program and on creating privacy on the east and west sides of the house and transparency on the north and south. Sidewalls functioning as both privacy walls and art walls reinforced this concept.

Entering the house, one understands the gallery as a linear columned space that connects the two and one-half story front entry hall to the rear stair. The front stair connects the lower entry level to the main living level, one story above. The entry space establishes, under a curved, segmented roof form, the volumetric aesthetic of the house.

The entry space engages one vertically and horizontally—vertically in section, with the entry stair balcony and upper roof, and horizontally, through the gallery to the back stair—revealing the diagram of the house. The horizontal connection is always land-driven and the vertical connection is always view-driven.

As the house engages the land and steps up the hill, horizontal spaces are created and the house becomes extended as a series of pavilions that are interconnected rather than consolidated. The conscious manipulation of floor planes allows the overviewing of one space from another. These subtle vertical shifts are part of the decompositional vocabulary that clarifies the idea of the house as a series of interconnected fragments.

The front building engages the ground with a garage and entry. The second level, accessed by an outdoor stair from the entry court as well as a service drive and court from the side street, contains the breakfast room and kitchen which overview Lake Zurich and the town of Zumikon.

This building is connected to the main house by a horizontal pavilion. On the ground floor (below grade), the art gallery is integrated into the entry sequence of the house, making it experiential and obligatory in the most positive sense. It is impossible to enter or leave the house without encountering the art.

On the second floor, the dining room serves as a transparent mediating space between the natural topography of the fields to the east and the man-made courtyard/roof terrace to the west. The stainless steel ceiling of the dining space, an inverted triangular section, plays against expectation by focusing the center of the room on the table and emphasizing the glass sidewalls. The glass block floor, which brings natural light into the art gallery below, and the concrete columns articulate the circulation zone.

A three-story cylindrical form, which is sliced and eroded, marks the intersection of the horizontal pavilion and the main house. The cylinder contains the terminal space of the gallery on the ground floor, the music room/library (overlooking the dining room) on the second floor, and the master bedroom on the third floor. Off the master bedroom, the roof of the dining room becomes a garden terrace, planted with annual flowers. It reestablishes, in the modernist tradition, the connection between occupied land and the building. This area is part of an integrated circulation system of terraces and outdoor spaces which brings one from the lower street level entry court up through the three levels of the house.

The cylinder is the formal device that allows the main house to rotate 90 degrees, forming the back side of the terrace. Instead of simply making an L-shaped building that turns a corner, the cylinder becomes a critical, spatial recognition of that intersection.

Rotated from the music room/library, the double-height living space meets the intersection of the rear stair and horizontal gallery, and opens toward the main terrace and the view of Lake Zurich and the Alps beyond. It is the interior space that is in scale with both the terrace and the view. Its back wall, which accommodates the fireplace—a sculptural anchor to the space, both wall-engaged and floating, and alternative focus to the view across the terrace—is also the front wall to the children's house.

The Bechtler children had all expressed a desire to have their own domain—their own public as well as private spaces. The resolution was to create their house as a distinct element, integrated into the composition, but accessed as a separate vertical building. This was accomplished by using the rear stair, which connects all levels, but engages the children's house at the half landings, physically and psychologically separating them from the main public and adult levels.

The children have their own entrance as well as their own interconnection to the main terrace through two balconies. These balconies are integrated into the pool house building, again reinforcing the children's house as separate, but part of a whole.

At the lowest half level, off the art gallery, is the double height playroom. This space engages two floors of the children's house, manipulating the volume to create a sectional hierarchy and sequence. The upper portion of the back wall contains a large window which clarifies, internally, the overall site section and emphasizes the back to front transparency of the house.

Two bedrooms flank this space on the second level, and an additional three bedrooms are located on the third level. Each of these levels is connected by a corridor that overlooks the living room through punched windows that allow the children to see into the living room and to the view beyond. This transparency reveals the plan and section separation.

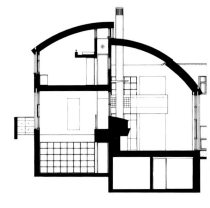

The curved segmented roofs are an elemental description of the volumes as well as a representation of the parti. The house is not read as a single object, but as a series of layered elements stepping down the hill, its fragments forming an assemblage or collage. It is a euphemistic village which anchors and establishes itself on the hill.

The opportunity to build this house of reinforced concrete with the level of craft that exists in Switzerland was compelling and influenced the form. This is literally a building of the ground, with a density and sense of permanence that is entirely different from that of our wood frame houses.

The materials used in this house—stucco on terra cotta for walls; lead-coated stainless steel for roofs; wood for windows and cabinetry; and limestone, sandstone and wood for floors—produced a selective aesthetic so precise and hierarchical that it establishes the primary reading of the building and creates spaces which are inherently self-decorative.

There is nothing automatic about the vocabulary of this building, either materially or formally. The curved, segmented roofs of the Opel House (Shelburne, Vermont, 1987) which are articulated as separate volumes, might have provided a sectional reference, but there the roofs, though segmented, are one form. Here the roof forms vary and are more dynamic due to the elements that intersect them, causing distortions and fragmentation.

This house consolidates the reductive essence of my parents' house (Amagansett, New York, 1965). It separates itself from the body of our work and represents a unique moment in my development. I was unintimidated, uncontaminated, energized and passionate about this work. Its realization has freed me from referential encumbrances and self-doubt. I am confident and whole again.

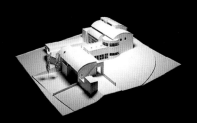

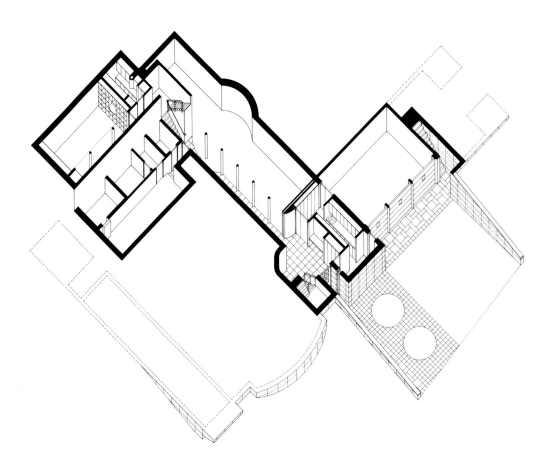

first level axonometric

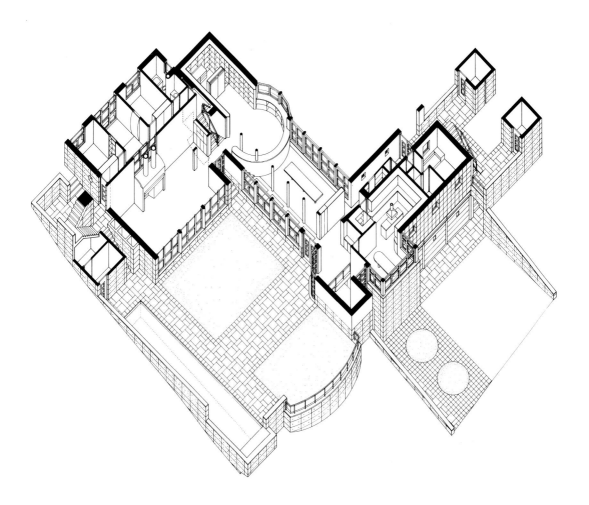

second level axonometric

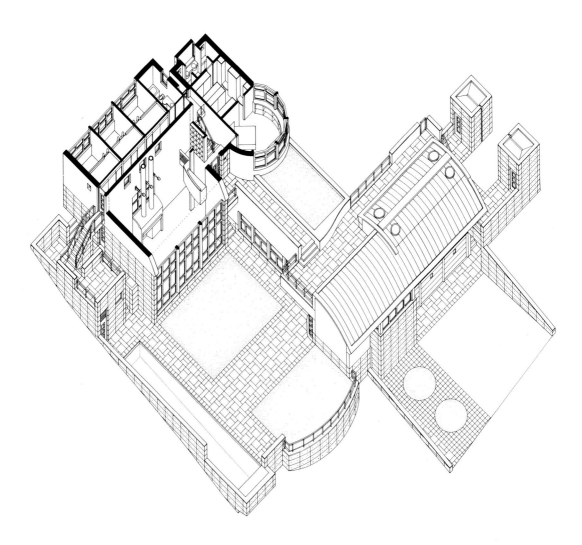

third level axonometric

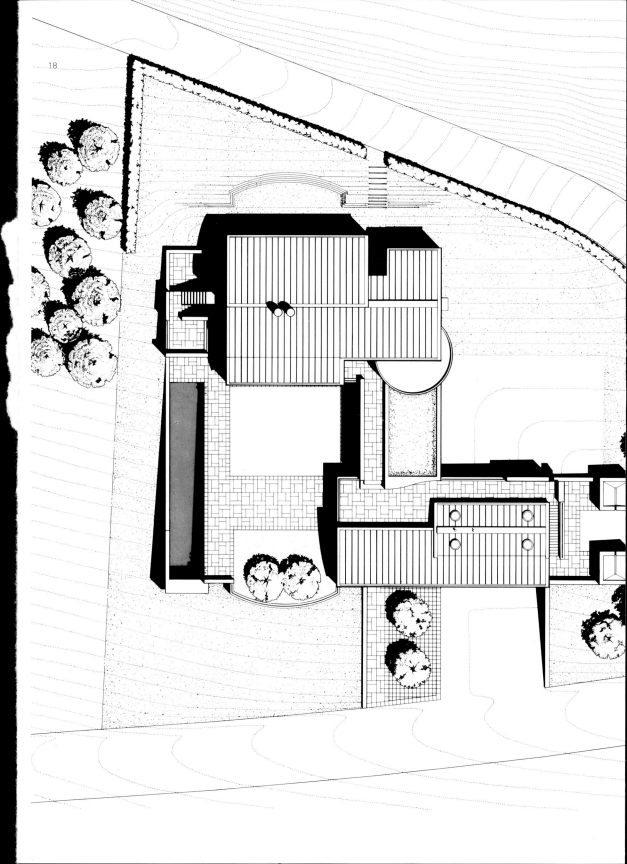

A   B   C

D

A   B   C

first level

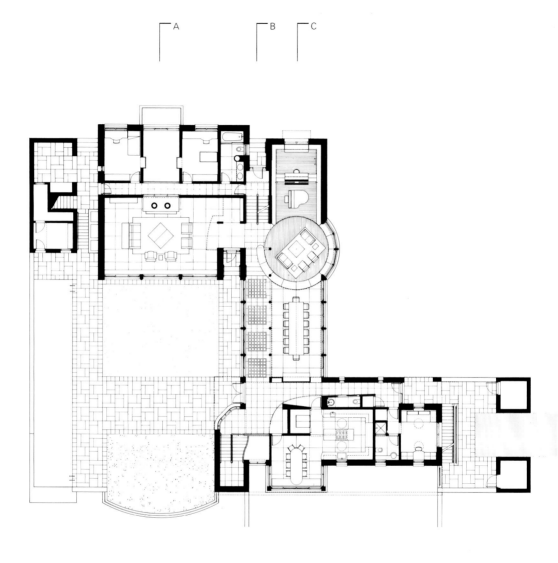

A B C

A B C

second level

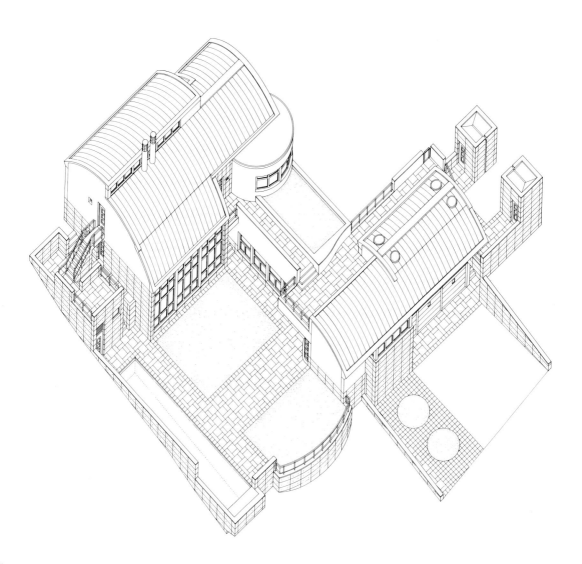

axonometric

south elevation

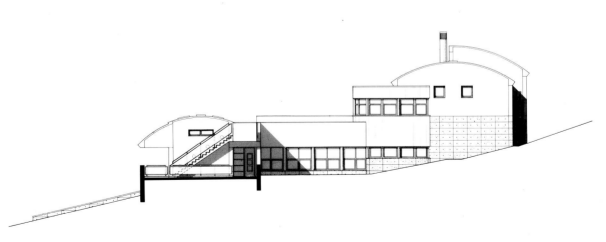

east elevation

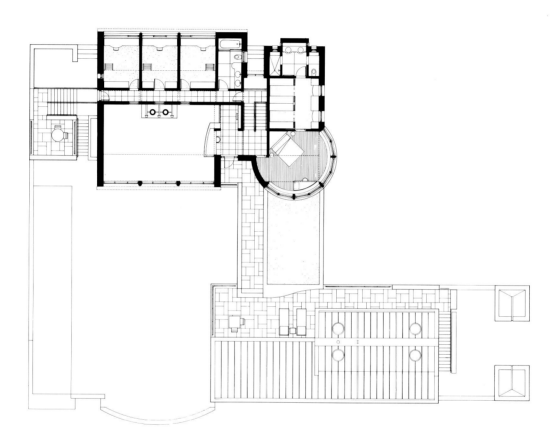

third level

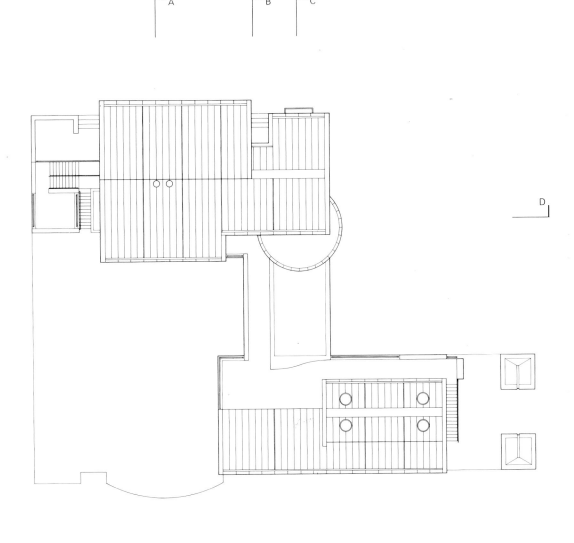

roof

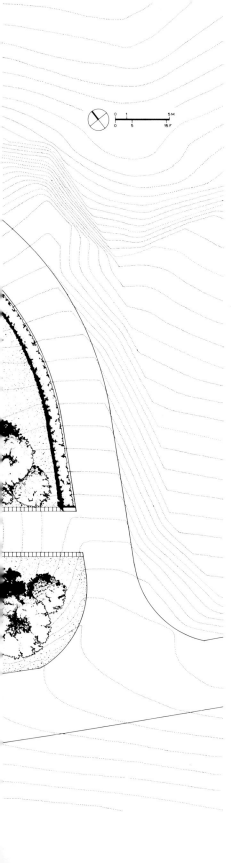

site plan

north elevation

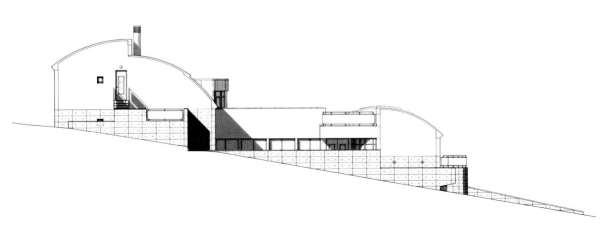

west elevation

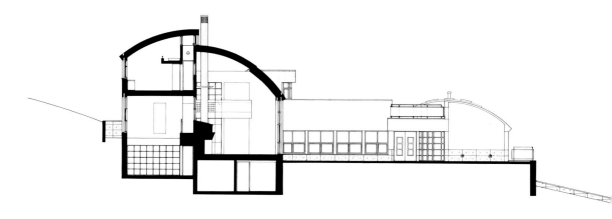

section A-A through terrace, living room, playroom, children's bedrooms

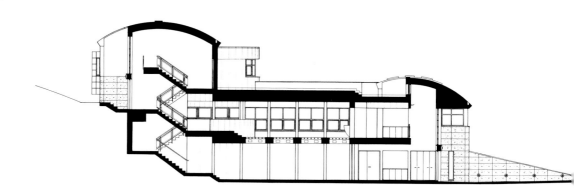

section B-B through entry, gallery, rear stair

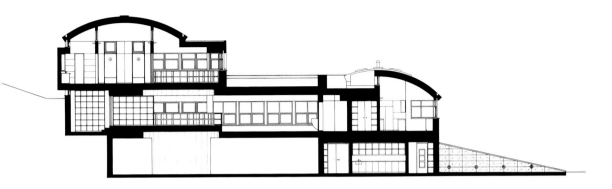

section C-C through gallery, dining area, library, study, master bedroom, dressing area

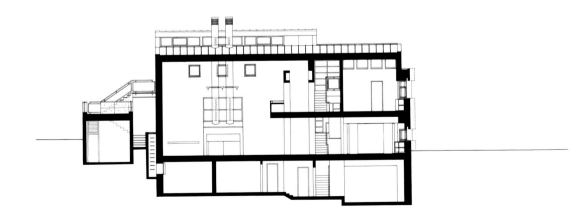

section D-D through living room, gallery, library, master bedroom

2,3 south facade

5

7 6

4

4,5 east facade 6 service entry drive from east 7 exterior stair to roof

8 detail of exterior stair to roof terrace **9** detail of east facade from service court

10 detail of south facade from service court 11 main entry, south facade

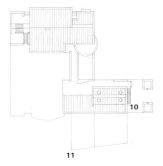

10

11

12 lower art gallery from entry 13 lower art gallery toward entry

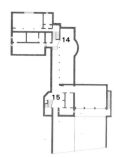

14 lower art gallery toward main stair **15** main stair

16 entry and second level from main stair landing **17** upper circulation gallery, dining space

WIND LINE ACROSS ENGLAND

A 130 MILE WALK IN 3½ DAYS FROM THE IRISH SEA COAST TO THE NORTH SEA COAST
THE WIND DIRECTION AT EACH COAST AND AT EVERY TEN MILES ALONG THE WAY

1986

18 detail of dining space **19** upper circulation gallery, dining space

20 kitchen **21** powder room

22 dining space toward library **23** music room/library

24 living space from library **25** living space toward study balcony

26 living space 27 living space toward study balcony

28 living space from study balcony **29** back stair from master bedroom landing **30** study balcony from master bedroom landing

28
29 30

31 master bedroom **32** exterior of master bedroom **33** roof garden outside master bedroom

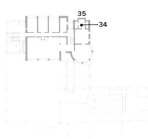

35
34

36

37

36 north facade 37 view through children's playroom and living room beyond

40 pool from upper terrace looking south to Zumikon, Lake Zurich and the Alps

40

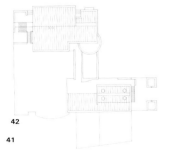

42

41

41 south facade 42 south facade and terrace

43 detail of south facade **44** detail of south terrace

43

44

45 pool terrace from southwest at dusk

Photography Credits

Richard Bryant, Arcaid pages 1, 2–3, 5, 9, 10, 11 (top), 12 (top); images 1–28, 31–35, 38–45

David Hirsch page 12 (bottom)

Mancia/Bodmer pages 8, 11 (bottom), 13; images 29, 30, 36, 37